STRESS
management 101

don colbert, m.d.

NELSON BOOKS
A Division of Thomas Nelson Publishers
Since 1798

www.thomasnelson.com

Published in Nashville, Tennessee, by Thomas Nelson, Inc.

Nelson Books titles may be purchased in bulk for educational, business, fund-raising, or sales promotional use. For information, please e-mail SpecialMarkets@ThomasNelson.com.

All Scripture references are from the NEW KING JAMES VERSION of the Bible. Copyright © 1982 by Thomas Nelson, Inc. Used by permission. All rights reserved.

Scripture quotations noted TLB are from *The Living Bible*, copyright © 1971. Used by permission of Tyndale House Publishers, Inc., Wheaton, Illinois 60189. All rights reserved.

Scripture quotations noted NASB are from the NEW AMERICAN STANDARD BIBLE ®, copyright © The Lockman Foundation 1960, 1962, 1963, 1968, 1971, 1972, 1973, 1975, 1977, 1995. Used by permission.

Library of Congress Cataloging-in-Publication Data

Colbert, Don.
    Stress management 101 / Don Colbert.
      p. cm.
    Includes bibliographical references.
    ISBN 0-7852-8795-7 (hardcover)
    1. Stress (Psychology) 2. Stress management. 3. Stress (Psychology)—Religious aspects—Christianity. I. Title.
  RA785.C64 2006
   616.9'8—dc22
   2006019089

Printed in the United States of America
06 07 08 09 WOR 6 5 4 3 2 1

Contents

Introduction

According to the American Institute of Stress, between 75 and 90 percent of all visits to primary-care physicians result from *stress-related disorders.*[1] The first signs of stress tend to be tension headaches, digestive-tract problems, and skin eruptions. Ironically, these conditions merely add another layer of stress.

If we don't treat the core causes of stress, the symptoms may become chronic. New, deeper symptoms can arise such as sleeplessness, weight loss or gain, muscle aches (especially back and neck pain), general lethargy or feelings of exhaustion, sluggish thinking, and lack of get-up-and-go or ambition.

If we continue to ignore the core stressors, the chronic

symptoms can become outright disease—the kinds that require surgery, chemotherapy and radiation therapy, and heavy-duty medications. Each of these treatments, of course, is also a stress-producer!

Stress upon stress upon stress—and all the while, the body doesn't differentiate what caused the stress in the first place. All the body knows is that it is experiencing stress.

HOW STRESS AFFECTS THE BODY

Stress is mental or physical tension, strain, or pressure. Stress reactions are the ways in which our bodies process and release both the emotions and the negative physical elements we experience in life. Through the years, scientific studies linking the emotions and disease have produced an impressive body of research. Here are some of the findings:

- Certain emotions release hormones, such as adrenaline and cortisol, into the physical body that, in turn, cause a damaging effect on the body and can trigger the development of a host of diseases.

- Researchers have directly and scientifically linked emotions to hypertension, cardiovascular disease, and diseases related to the immune system. Studies have also highly correlated emotions with infections, allergies, and autoimmune diseases.

- Specifically, research has linked emotions such as depression to an increased risk of developing cancer and heart disease. Emotions such as anxiety and fear have shown a direct tie to heart palpitations, mitral valve prolapse, irritable bowel syndrome, and tension headaches, as well as other diseases.

- The body perceives stress created by good experiences in the same way it perceives stress created by negative experiences. Even so, certain emotional states—such as rage, unforgiveness, depression, worry, and grief—are much more damaging than others.

- A stress response is good only if one experiences it over the short term. A chronic stress response is *always* damaging to the body.

WHAT WE CAN DO

So, what can we do? We must learn how to "turn off" the stress response and cope with stress.

Stress is not about events and experiences nearly so much as it is about our *perception* of the circumstances that occur in our lives. Our stress level has to do with what we *believe*. Because we can choose what we believe or think, we have the ability to choose how we will respond to the stressful events and circumstances in our lives. In other words, we can *choose* a less stressful way of life!

This book outlines seven steps you can take to successfully manage stress and live a healthier life. This plan is based on God's Word, nutrition, exercise, and common sense. It teaches how you can be genuinely happy without the use of chemicals, medications, or mood-altering substances. By concentrating on emotional well-being, you will live not only with less stress and anxiety but also with more joy, better physical health, and a peace that passes all understanding.

Choose today to begin taking steps toward a healthier, less stressful life!

ONE

Choose Your Attitudes

Victor Frankl was a psychiatrist and Jew who was imprisoned by the Nazis in the death camps of World War II Germany. In his book *Man's Search for Meaning*, he tells how he came to the realization that his own *choices,* not his circumstances, defined his identity. No matter how horrifying the environment in which he lived, and no matter how much humiliation and degradation others heaped upon him, he was still in control of how he chose to respond. The same is true for each of us.

No event can change you on the inside unless you allow it to do so. No person can cause you to respond in a particular way on the inside unless you choose to react that way. The freedom to forge your own opinions, ideas, attitudes, and choices rests solely and uniquely with *you.*

THE POWER OF YOUR ATTITUDE

In his book *Strengthening Your Grip,* Charles Swindoll writes that the most significant decision we can make on a daily basis is our choice of attitude. He asserts that attitude is more important than one's past, education, bankroll, successes or failures, circumstances, or position.

To some extent, all damaging, stress-producing emotions derive from our attitudes and reactions. And attitudes are something we can control. You can choose how you will think and feel about any circumstance, event, or relationship in your life. You can choose to a great extent how you deal with grief, resentment, bitterness, shame, jealousy, guilt, fear, worry, depression, anger, hostility, and all other emotional situations that readily trigger physical responses.

The first step you need to take toward less stress and better health is to reflect upon your own attitudes. Own up to the attitudes you have. Ask yourself, "Is this the way I *want* to think and believe?"

COMMUNICATING WITH YOUR HEART

Research has shown that the heart sends messages to the brain that appear to be capable of affecting an individual's behavior. The ultimate "real you" is a composite of what your heart tells your brain, your brain tells your heart, and your will decides to believe, say, and do. Therefore, two of the most powerful antidotes for damaging emotions are these:

- Communicating with your own heart
- Learning to live in the love that flows from the heart

King David talked to his own heart: "Why are you cast down, O my soul? And why are you disquieted within me? Hope in God, for I shall yet praise Him for the help of His countenance" (Ps. 42:5).

You may feel silly "talking to your heart," but do it

anyway! Just venting the words will do two things: it will clarify to you what you truly are feeling, and you will give release to some of your pent-up emotions.

Notice that David did not only admit to himself that he was downcast in his soul. He went on to tell himself, "Hope in God!" He went on to say of his chosen course of action, "I shall yet praise Him." Furthermore, David said he would praise God for the "help of His countenance." He praised God not for a specific act that God had taken or would take, but for the sheer help of knowing that God was present with him.

These steps David took in his "soul conversation" are very important. You can follow his lead:

1. Voice aloud what you are feeling.
2. Voice aloud your decision to hope in God.
3. Voice aloud your decision to praise God for who He is in your life. Acknowledge His near presence and His continual availability to you.

David went on to voice these same concepts to God in prayer: "O my God, my soul is cast down within me; therefore I will remember You" (Ps. 42:6).

Turn from speaking to yourself to speaking to God. Admit to God your feelings. Cast your concerns on Him and voice your decision to trust Him.

Effective communication with your heart requires that you become quiet and do your best to turn off the constant mental tapes that are playing in your head, to turn away from the remembrance of painful hurts and frustrations. Many people find it helpful to focus on events or people in their lives that have brought joy, love, happiness, and peace. Also, develop an attitude of gratitude and appreciation by focusing on all the good things in your life rather than on the traumas or negative things that have happened.

Ask your heart:

- "What is it that you are *really* feeling?"
- "*Why* are you feeling this way?"
- "What good thing are you *really* hoping for?"

The heart speaks in the quietest of voices. You may feel a little internal "nudge" or a sense of warning. Give your heart the benefit of communicating its wisdom to your brain.

Spend a few minutes every day listening to your heart. And then:

- Speak words of encouragement to your heart.
- Voice words of appreciation for life's blessings.
- Recall events in your life when you experienced tremendous joy, peace, or love.
- Speak words of acknowledgment about personal accomplishments, reflections of noble character, or acts of kindness or ministry to others. If nobody else openly acknowledges the goodness of the Lord manifested in and through your life, acknowledge this to yourself.
- Read aloud the Word of God to your heart. I recommend that you place an emphasis on the words of Jesus in the New Testament (especially 1, 2, and 3 John) and the book of Proverbs.
- Voice your heartfelt prayers and concerns to God, beginning with a time of giving God thanks for all He has done, is doing, and has promised to do. Speak your praise to God for who He is.
- Give God your frustrations, fears, and anger. Turn over your anxious thoughts to Him. The Bible tells

us, "Let [God] have all your worries and cares, for he is always thinking about you and watching everything that concerns you" (1 Peter 5:7 TLB).

- Ask God to fill your heart with His love and presence. Openly invite the Holy Spirit to impart to you the fruit of His presence in you, which includes "love, joy, peace, longsuffering, kindness, goodness, faithfulness, gentleness, self-control" (Gal. 5:22–23).

When you experience God in your heart, you will also experience His love. The Bible says the two are inseparable: "He who does not love does not know God, for God is love" (1 John 4:8).

THE HEART COMMUNICATES TO THE BODY

As you learn to communicate with your own heart and release positive feelings of love to your own soul, your heart in turn communicates this message of well-being to your body through the release of helpful hormones and neurotransmitters. The most powerful channel of heart communication to the body, however, is through the heart's electromagnetic field, which is significantly greater in strength than the electromagnetic field the brain produces.

In addition, heart rates send varying messages to the brain and body. When a person is fearful, for example, the heart speeds up, sending a signal to the entire body. When a person is content and happy, heart rate slows, telling the entire nervous system that the person is feeling good.

A seventeenth-century clock maker discovered a fascinating principle called "entrainment," which we can apply to the heart. In a grouping of clocks, the largest clock with the strongest rhythm will pull the other pendulums into sync with itself. Likewise, the heart, which is the strongest biological oscillator in the body, has the ability to pull every other bodily system into its own rhythm. When the heart is at peace or filled with love, it communicates harmony to the entire body. Conversely, when negative emotions have triggered the heart to beat in an irregular way—harder or faster—the heart communicates the very opposite of peace to the other organs of the body.

Spiritually speaking, when you experience God's peace,

the heart communicates peace to every fiber of your being. Each and every organ experiences that rest. When you experience God's love and the love of other people, the heart communicates that love to your mind and your entire body. When love fills your heart, your entire body takes something of an emotional plunge into healing.

The greatest Physician and Healer who ever lived, Jesus Christ, explained this phenomenon in His own terms: "It is not what goes into a man that defiles a man, but what comes out of his heart" (Matt. 15:17–18, author's paraphrase).

AN ATTITUDE OF GRATITUDE

In Philippians 4:4, Paul says, "Rejoice in the Lord always. Again I will say, rejoice!" Paul wrote this while in prison. Though judgment was imminent and conditions were harsh, he had an attitude of gratitude. Where the mind goes, the health of your body will follow. If your mind is full of anxiety, fear, anger, depression, and guilt, it chronically stimulates the stress response, which opens the door for disease to enter the body. I believe that many diseases, such as autoimmune disease and cancer, are directly related to deadly emotions. It's like deadly emotions are flipping a self-destruct switch in your body.

Start practicing appreciation and thanksgiving on a daily basis. Compliment your spouse, children, coworkers, and friends regularly. Begin to compliment or give words of appreciation to strangers such as waiters, store clerks, toll-booth operators, and people you come in contact with daily. Instead of pointing out their faults, begin to see their strengths. It will do your heart—and your body—good!

TWO

Change Your Way of Thinking

Years ago, a *Pogo* comic strip became popular because it so accurately and succinctly described the human condition. Pogo declared, "We have met the enemy and they are us!" Sadly, we are often our own worst enemies.

NEGATIVE THINKING AND FALSE BELIEFS

When we are stressed, depressed, angry, anxious, or feeling guilty, we are more prone to misinterpret events and think in distorted ways. One distorted thought tends to lead to another and, before long, we are trapped in a downward spiral. We begin voicing negative statements such as, "Nothing ever goes right for me," or "I just can't do anything right." This is called distortional thinking.

Dr. Albert Ellis, a renowned psychologist in the 1950s, believed that damaging emotions arise from three negative and false beliefs:

False Belief #1: I must do well.
False Belief #2: You must treat me well.
False Belief #3: The world must be easy.[1]

A sane, rational, and potentially positive person is someone who recognizes that nobody does well all the time. Everybody has faults, foibles, and flaws. The healthy perception is that people at times are not going to treat us well, and the world at times is not going to be easy.

A person who practices distorted thinking must learn to change the way he thinks and interprets events. This practice has been called cognitive therapy. A significant part of the therapy involves changing the way a person talks. In response to a negatively perceived situation, a person might be taught to say, "This didn't go well, but most of the time things do go well," or "I may have failed in this, but overall I've enjoyed successes in my life."

In his book *Feeling Good,* renowned psychiatrist Dr. David Burns explains that several principles are vital for gaining control over false beliefs and negative thinking:

- Thoughts create moods. Thoughts can lead to anger, hostility, depression, sadness, anxiety, fear, shame, or guilt.
- The thoughts of a person who feels depressed are dominated by negativity.
- Negative thoughts that trigger damaging emotions nearly always contain irrational, twisted, or unrealistic thought patterns.

Dr. Burns has identified ten types of negative beliefs:

1. All-or-Nothing Thinking

The person who thinks this way sees everything in black or white terms. No shades of gray are possible. Perfectionists see their work as either perfect or worthless, whereas the healthy person sees spectrums, variations, and exceptions in nearly every area of life.

2. Overgeneralizations

This is the tendency to draw sweeping conclusions from very little evidence. For example, a man who is turned down by one woman after he asks for a date may draw the conclusion that all women will reject him and he will never get a date. The healthy thinker draws conclusions only after taking in a great deal of evidence.

3. Negative Mental Filter

This person filters out any bit of information that is positive or good. She just doesn't hear compliments or words of affirmation or praise. She hears only criticism. The healthy person hears both good and bad.

4. Disqualifying the Positive

This person hears the compliment but discounts it. He explains away words of affirmation or praise. For example, a person who is given a promotion may say, "I don't deserve this. They are just feeling sorry for me because I'm really such a loser." The healthy person receives compliments and praise and uses them to validate his own self-esteem.

5. Jumping to Conclusions

This person believes she knows at all times, with 100 percent accuracy, what other people are thinking about her. The healthy person assumes she isn't a mind reader.

6. Magnification (Catastrophizing) or Minimization

This person exaggerates the importance of isolated events or encounters. He may magnify his own emotions, mistakes, or imperfections. He minimizes, however, any success he may have. A healthy-thinking person maximizes the good points and minimizes the failures.

7. Emotional Reasoning

This person sees an outcome as directly flowing from her emotions. For example, the person may feel hopeless about passing an exam, so she doesn't show up to take it. The healthy person separates current feelings from future events.

8. "Should" Statements

This person has a rigid set of internal rules about what should, must, ought to, and has to be done. The healthy person knows and expresses the fact that there are very few hard-and-fast rules in life.

9. Labeling and Mislabeling

This person is likely to give himself or another person negative labels such as "stupid," "idiot," "imbecile," "loser," "jerk," or "pig." The healthy person avoids labels.

10. Personalization

This person blames himself for events over which he has no control or less control than he assumes. I've encountered a number of parents who blame themselves for their teenagers' experimentation with drugs. They become filled with guilt and self-judgment when the fact is, they need to hold the teenager accountable for his choices and behavior. The healthy person refuses to take responsibility or blame for someone else's freewill choices.

EXAMINE YOUR THOUGHT PATTERNS

The best way to address negative thinking patterns is to listen to yourself. Every time you hear yourself drawing a conclusion that may reflect any of Dr. Burns's ten thinking patterns—or anytime you hear yourself applying a label such as "stupid" to yourself—write it down.

I often encourage persons to write in a journal identifying statements about themselves after monitoring the way they refer to and talk about themselves.

Then I ask them to go back through those journal entries and write next to each label or each possibility of distorted thinking a verse or short passage from the Bible that addresses that perception.

Next, I ask them to confess to God that they have allowed themselves to develop distorted thinking. They have bought into lies. I encourage them to seek God's forgiveness and to ask God to set them free from the bondage that these lies have created in their souls. I encourage them to ask God to heal the damaged emotions and distorted thinking that they have developed.

Finally, I advise individuals to memorize the verses that they have written down in their journals. These are the foremost verses they are likely to need, and to quote, in order to keep negative thinking from continuing to take root.

TRANSFORMING TRUTHS

Let me share some of the verses from the Bible that I
believe have great transforming power when it comes to
distorted, negative thinking:

- I can do all things through Christ who strengthens
  me. (Phil. 4:13)
- Thanks be to God who always leads us in triumph
  in Christ. (2 Cor. 2:14)
- My God shall supply all your need according to
  His riches in glory by Christ Jesus. (Phil. 4:19)
- [Jesus said,] Do not intimidate anyone or accuse
  falsely, and be content with your wages. (Luke 3:14)
- Do not think it strange concerning the fiery trial
  which is to try you . . . but rejoice to the extent that
  you partake of Christ's sufferings, that when His
  glory is revealed, you may also be glad with exceed-
  ing joy. (1 Peter 4:12–13)

I encourage you to purchase a Bible promises book
that contains God's guarantees in the Bible, as well as a
concordance to look up verses related to key concepts or

words. Then begin replacing distorted thoughts with God's promises.

RENEWING YOUR MIND

Every person has some degree of distortional or negative thinking. The key to overcoming negative thought patterns—and to developing a mind that truly thinks as Christ Jesus thinks—is to confront distortional thinking continually with the truth of God. Seek to develop the ability to identify false thinking, recognize what kind of distortion is taking place, and then change the thought by replacing it with healthy, godly truth.

The apostle Paul challenged followers of Christ, "Do not be conformed to this world, but be transformed by the renewing of your mind, that you may prove what is that good and acceptable and perfect will of God" (Rom. 12:2). Part of experiencing a spiritual renewal in your mind is to make a conscious choice that you will change what you put into your mind, and therefore, change your thought patterns.

I have worked with countless people who have

discovered that once they made a sincere effort to tackle their distorted thought patterns, they had fewer bouts of depression, anxiety, anger, grief, shame, jealousy, and all other negative emotions that lead to stress. It isn't difficult to replace lies with God's truth. It just takes intentional and consistent effort . . . it takes the time and energy to find statements of God's truth and apply them to life's lies. Jesus promised, "If you abide in My word, you are My disciples indeed. And you shall know the truth, and the truth shall make you free" (John 8:31–32).

The Bible has this to say about the choices we make in our thought lives: "Finally, brethren, whatever is true, whatever is honorable, whatever is right, whatever is pure, whatever is lovely, whatever is of good repute, if there is any excellence and if anything worthy of praise, let your mind dwell on these things" (Phil. 4:8 NASB).

Choose to think about those things that evoke positive emotions within you. Focus on them. Emphasize them. Reflect often on them. They are your best line of defense against damaging, stress-producing thoughts.

THREE

Choose to Forgive

Those who forgive are those who choose to forgive. There's nothing automatic, unintentional, or happenstance about forgiveness. It is a choice and an act of the will.

Those who choose to forgive are those who decide to give up resentment and the desire to punish. They actually cancel the debt they believe another person owes them.

UNDERSTANDING FORGIVENESS

One of the reasons many people find it difficult to forgive is that they have a false understanding of forgiveness.

Forgiveness is not based on finding some redeeming quality that makes a person worth forgiving. Forgiveness comes solely from your desire to forgive for the sake of forgiving. Nobody who intentionally harms another person truly deserves forgiveness from the person he has hurt. Even so, it's far better to forgive and to live in the resulting emotional freedom and health than to suffer the consequences of failing to forgive.

Forgiveness does not require minimizing pain. To forgive does not mean that a person is saying, "This didn't matter," or "This wasn't a huge wrong committed against me." Rather, it is saying, "I choose no longer to hold this feeling of unforgiveness toward the person who hurt me."

Forgiveness does not mean letting a person off the hook so that no justice is required. A forgiving person can still require a person to face legal penalties for a crime committed. Forgiveness means putting another person squarely in the hands of God, canceling the debt, refusing to think or talk about the hurt, and allowing God to work His justice in that person's life. It is trusting God to deal with the offending person, the hurtful situation, and the memories of terrible events. It is trusting God to heal the wound inside. In the end, God's justice—coupled

with His mercy, love, and desire to redeem and forgive—
will always be far superior to ours.

Some contend that emotional wounds heal over time.
I have rarely seen that to be the case. Extremely painful
events in childhood can hurt just as much seventy or
eighty years later. Forgiving deep emotional wounds and
seriously damaging offenses is nearly always a process
requiring both time and intentional effort. We must never
lose sight of the fact that forgiveness is a matter of the will.

Forgiveness is an act of strength. It takes little inner
fortitude to harbor anger, resentment, or hate. It takes a
great deal of courage to lay down one's anger and seek to
walk away in peace. Gandhi once said, "The weak can
never forgive. Forgiveness is the attribute of the strong."

Colossians 3:13 says, "Bearing with one another, and
forgiving one another, if anyone has a complaint against
another; even as Christ forgave you, so you also *must* do."
The person who can't forgive has forgotten the great debt
for which they were forgiven. When you get a revelation
that Jesus delivered you from spiritual death, hell, and
the grave, you will forgive others unconditionally.

Finally, forgiveness is not the same thing as reconciliation. You can forgive a person if he doesn't forgive

you, but reconciliation always requires the wills of both parties involved. That's an important distinction to make.

You may forgive but find the other person unwilling to reconcile. If that happens, know that you have done your part. Leave behind the negative emotions between you and that person. Trust God to do His work in the other person's life in His timing and using His methods.

Also recognize that there are some situations in which reconciliation may not be advisable, such as in cases of domestic abuse, stalking, violent behavior, or sexual abuse of a child. If that is the case, don't beat yourself up emotionally for a failure to reconcile. God requires forgiveness of you, not a reuniting with a person who has hurt you or who exhibits ongoing destructive behavior.

BENEFITS OF FORGIVENESS

Forgiveness enables a person to release buried anger, resentment, bitterness, shame, grief, regret, guilt, hate, and other toxic emotions that hide deep in the soul and make a person ill—both emotionally and physically. A permeating sense of peace that blankets a person's entire being commonly accompanies true forgiveness.

Forgiveness releases layers of hurt and heals the raw, jagged edges of emotional pain. Saying "I forgive" is like taking an emotional shower—forgiveness cleanses and frees the entrapped soul.

Forgiveness leads to an ability to love. Some contend that forgiveness flows from a loving heart, but the opposite is actually true: love flows from a forgiving heart. It's virtually impossible to love a person against whom you are holding a grudge, with whom you have had a painful encounter, or from whom you have experienced rejection or emotional pain. Forgiveness opens the door to love.

Finally, forgiveness leads to better health. Scientific studies have demonstrated that developing an ability to forgive decreases the risk of heart disease and other physical complaints. Those who learn to forgive are better able to control their emotions and are generally less angry and upset. Learning to forgive has also been shown to decrease depression and increase feelings of physical vitality and general well-being.

The healthiest people among us seem to be those who

laugh easily, forget unpleasant events quickly, and are quick to forgive even the gravest offenses. This kind of childlikeness keeps a person unencumbered emotionally and spiritually, and in the end, unencumbered physically. It is no mystery to me as a physician that the Bible teaches us to become "as little children" in our relationship with God and in our ability to forgive, believe, and express our faith (Matt. 18:3).

CONSEQUENCES OF UNFORGIVENESS

If you choose not to forgive someone, I guarantee that your emotions of resentment and hatred will continue to poison your system in ways that are just as dangerous as your taking in a literal poison. Not only will your body suffer, but also your mind, spirit, and general well-being.

In failing to forgive, you really are hurting only yourself. Unforgiveness rarely hurts the person you offended. Most of the people you are unwilling to forgive don't even realize you are upset with them. Many may be completely unaware of having offended you in any way.

FORGIVENESS IS A PROCESS

We often need to express and feel forgiveness in a step-by-step progression. I see the process as having these stages:

1. Admit You Have Been Wounded

Before you can forgive, you need to openly admit to yourself that events, words, situations, or attitudes have hurt or wounded you emotionally and spiritually—in your past or your current life. Admit that the offense has occurred, no matter how slight you think it is, and acknowledge that what happened to you brought you emotional pain.

2. Accept God's Forgiveness in Your Life

According to the Bible, the only way a person can fully forgive another person is to know first that God has forgiven him. God's forgiveness of us forms the basis for our ability to forgive others (see Matt. 6:12, 14–15 and Luke 6:37).

If you believe you had any part whatsoever in the wrong committed against you, confess that to God and receive His forgiveness. And then, forgive yourself. If you can't forgive yourself knowing that God has forgiven you, then generally you can't forgive others. Accept the fact that God's forgiveness is complete. In fact, the Bible tells us that what God forgives, God forgets. (See Ps. 103:12.)

If you believe you had absolutely no part whatsoever in the wrong committed against you, you will still be wise to ask God to forgive you for harboring any unforgiveness against the person. Ask God to heal you of the painful memories you have of the event or circumstances in which you were hurt.

3. Openly Release the Offender to God's Hands

Some time ago I talked with a person who told me that when he counsels people who need to forgive, he hands them a small rubbery toy. He tells them to hold on to that toy with all their strength, using both hands. And then he says, "Now, if you are ready to forgive, I want to lead you in a prayer. I want you to see the person you are forgiving as being like that little rubber toy you are squeezing so hard. That's the way unforgiveness works in your soul. You are holding on to this person, and the time has come to release him. As we pray, I want you to let go of this person and place him in the hands of God. Let go of the toy. And then, turn your palms up and receive God's love. Lay your hands over your heart."

I asked, "What happens when you do this?"

He said, "At times, the person can hardly let go. He thinks it will be easy, but it is very difficult. Sometimes when the person does let go, he begins to sob—very often for quite a while. And it's only after all the tears are out that a person finds he can truly receive God's love in his own heart."

4. Ask God to Help You

Ask God to help you forgive the person who has offended you. He knows far more about forgiveness than any human being! Trust Him to impart to you the ability to forgive fully and freely.

5. Voice Your Forgiveness

Focus on the name of a person who has hurt you, harshly judged you, falsely labeled you, or in any way brought you feelings of emotional pain or distress. Speak that person's name in the blank provided in the following prayer:

Heavenly Father, I choose today to forgive _____
of any offense committed against me, whether knowingly

or unknowingly. I release to You all of the memories and toxic emotions of unforgiveness that may be buried in my heart. I declare before You right now that this event, situation, or circumstance of offense against me is now dead forever. Heal me, Father. Help me to move forward in the freedom and strength of forgiveness. Fill me with Your love, joy, and peace.

In my experience of having patients pray this prayer, I have found that some people begin to experience a flood of memories. They think they are forgiving just one offense, but suddenly five new offenses take its place. I encourage the person, as he recalls each new offense, to repeat the forgiveness prayer. At times, I've had a person repeat this prayer a dozen times or more.

Many times we have to take an initial step of forgiveness to start the forgiveness process. Sometimes we must repeat the act of forgiving each time a new set of painful memories comes to the surface.

6. Consider Whether You Need to Ask or Grant Forgiveness to the Offending Person

There may be times when your process of forgiveness is

complete only when you ask another person to forgive you. Sometimes you need to go to a person who has asked for your forgiveness—and from whom you have withheld it—and grant the forgiveness requested. Forgiveness is the foremost gift we can give to another person.

PARTIAL VS. FULL FORGIVENESS

A person who partially forgives another may experience a decrease in negative feelings but gains no genuine emotional freedom or peace. Partial forgiveness tends to happen in the head. A person mouths the words and thinks he has forgiven, but deep inside, memories of the offense still trigger pangs of pain and resentful feelings. He feels little or no affection toward the person who wounded him.

Full forgiveness, in contrast, happens in the heart. It allows a total release of all negative feelings once directed toward the offender. This type of forgiveness is cleansing and cathartic.

If you are still working at forgiveness, be encouraged that release *will come* if you continue to ask God to help you forgive.

FORGIVING YOURSELF

Perhaps the most difficult act of forgiveness is forgiving ourselves. To be truly cleansed and to move forward into emotional well-being, we must take a look at our own lives and, in those areas where we see we have failed, ask for God's forgiveness.

Once we have asked God for forgiveness, we need to truly believe that God has forgiven us. The Bible promises, "If we confess our sins, He is faithful and just to forgive us our sins and to cleanse us from all unrighteousness" (1 John 1:9).

Then we need to forgive ourselves. Failing to do this can result in shame, remorse, guilt, and regret. Daily, you must love yourself, accept yourself, and forgive yourself. Never compare, condemn, or criticize yourself. You are not stupid, dumb, or a failure. You may have done something dumb, but you are not dumb. You are identified with Christ and need to renew your mind with God's Word every day.

Some people find it very difficult to forgive themselves for the abuse they have showered on spouses or children, for extramarital affairs they have had, for abortions, drug or alcohol abuse, or for squandering the family's money on gambling. The apostle Paul wrote these words of encouragement: "One thing I do, forgetting those things which are behind and reaching forward to those things which are ahead, I press toward the goal for the prize of the upward call of God in Christ Jesus" (Phil. 3:13–14).

It isn't enough that a person simply says, "Oh well, that was in the past. I'll forget that and go forward." To do that is to dismiss the vitally important step of forgiveness. Confession of sin and experiencing God's forgiveness are vital in being able truly to forget the past.

At the same time, once we have confessed our sins to God and received His forgiveness, we should press toward the goal that lies ahead. This pressing on includes an active, intentional act of goal-setting and of looking to the future with hope, fully believing, "I can do all things through Christ who strengthens me" (Phil. 4:13). You are not a failure or a loser, but as a Christian, you are a new creature; old things have passed away and all things have been made new. (See 2 Corinthians 5:17.) You are the righteousness of God in Christ. (See 2 Corinthians 5:21.) Get a revelation of who you are in Christ and begin to see yourself as God sees you.

LIVING IN A STATE OF FORGIVENESS

Choose to live in a state of forgiveness. The only way to do that is to ask God's forgiveness daily and to forgive yourself daily and all those who may have harmed, ridiculed, persecuted, rejected, criticized, or maligned you, or who otherwise trespassed on your peace of mind and your personal faith.

If you are struggling with forgiveness, I encourage you to read and study all the Bible has to say about it. Use a concordance to find the many references. The Bible has a number of stories and teachings about forgiveness.

- Joseph's story is a wonderful account of a young man who experienced repeated injustices; but in the end, he came to believe that all of the injustices served God's ultimately positive purposes in his life and in the lives of his family members. (See Gen. 37–45.)
- The parable of the prodigal son is a story of a father's generous forgiveness. (See Luke 15:11–32.)
- The parable of a servant who owed an enormous debt is a story about our need to forgive. (See Matt. 18:23–35.)

Ongoing forgiveness keeps damaging emotions from building up. Daily forgiveness is my foremost prescription for a person's total mental, emotional, spiritual, and physical health. Most patients that come to my office for chronic diseases need to go through forgiveness therapy. Such therapy consists of intense, prayer-filled counseling, which helps people walk through their greatest pains and allows them to cancel the debts they feel others owe them. It is such a simple yet profound therapy that has released many from their physical disease.

FOUR

Lighten Up!

The Bible says, "A merry heart does good, like medicine" (Prov. 17:22). As a physician who has literally prescribed laughter to patients who were suffering from physical and emotional pain, I have seen the truth of that verse borne out many times.

LAUGHTER IS GOOD MEDICINE

Studies have demonstrated the health and healing benefits of laughter. Laughter has been found to boost the immune system and reduce dangerous stress hormones, such as adrenaline and cortisol, in the body. Laughter's ability to reduce levels of cortisol is especially important. Cortisol is the dangerous stress hormone that, once elevated for extended periods of time, can act like acid in the body. It especially affects the brain, eventually causing memory loss. It is hard to lower cortisol medically once its level rises. Laughter truly is a good prescription!

Studies also have shown that laughter can lower blood pressure. In 2000, a team of researchers at the University of Maryland reported that individuals who used humor in their speech patterns often were less likely to suffer a heart attack than those who didn't. Still other researchers have found that people with a good sense of humor experience overall "less stress and better health."[1]

Laughter also has been found to help the functioning of the brain, allowing a person to use both sides of the brain simultaneously. Some research has shown that people are more creative in problem-solving after they perceive something as humorous. Other studies suggest that laughter helps increase the flexibility and creativity of thought.

The Healing Effects of Laughter

Norman Cousins, journalist and former editor of the *Saturday Review,* conducted a personal experiment with the healing benefits of laughter after developing an extremely painful disease of the connective tissue called ankylosing spondylitis. Cousins began watching funny movies in order to make himself laugh to see if laughter influenced his level of pain. Over time, he noticed that laughing before going to bed helped him sleep.

As the laughter therapy continued, Cousins noticed something else begin to happen. He was getting well! The inflammation in his body started to decrease after a session of laughter, and, over time, it returned to normal. Cousins indeed got well. He later wrote a book about his remarkable story, titled *Anatomy of an Illness.*

The healing power of laughter became a life passion for Cousins, who worked with Loma Linda University in conducting research on how laughter affects stress hormones and the immune system. Cousins spent the final twelve years of his life at UCLA Medical School, where he worked as an adjunct professor and set up a humor task force to conduct clinical research on laughter. This research has now been ongoing for twenty years at the

UCLA Norman Cousins Center for Psychoneuro-immunology, which is presently conducting research under the umbrella title of "Rx Laughter Study."

In this study, medical personnel are showing extremely ill children funny videos, cartoons, television shows, and films to see how laughter impacts their immune systems. Researchers are finding that children are healing faster and with less pain (refer to www.rxlaughter.org).

Laughter Is Good Exercise

One researcher has concluded that laughter's effect in the body is similar to a good aerobic exercise. Dr. William Fry, Jr. has researched the potential therapeutic properties of laughter and humor for more than thirty years. In his book *Make 'Em Laugh,* he contends that laughter ventilates the lungs and leaves the muscles, nerves, and heart warm and relaxed—the very same benefits of aerobic exercise. Cousins writes in *Anatomy of an Illness* that laughter is like "internal jogging." Others have likened the effects of laughter to those of a deep massage.

As with aerobic exercise, laughter temporarily speeds up the heart rate, increases blood pressure and breathing, expands circulation, and enhances the flow of oxygen in and out of the body. A good belly laugh also exercises the upper torso, lungs, and heart, as well as the shoulders, arms, abdomen, diaphragm, and legs. Laughing one hundred to two hundred times a day is equal to ten minutes of rowing or jogging. Some researchers contend that twenty seconds of belly laughter is equivalent to three minutes of working out on a rowing machine. In my opinion, bring on the laughter!

START WITH A SMILE

Laughter is infectious. In most cases, it is a spontaneous response. Few people can force themselves to begin a belly laugh. How, then, can a person learn to laugh? By choosing to smile.

One of the first expressions an infant makes is a smile, and this occurs sometimes as early as six weeks of age. Smiles are built into you—it's up to you to choose to express them!

While smiling may not be quite as therapeutic as laughing, smiling does have physical benefits in the body. Facial expressions are connected neurologically to emotional states. Not only do laughter and smiling *reflect* an inner emotional state, but these expressions can *trigger* an emotional state. A smile on the face can cause a response in the heart. Research has shown that facial expressions can even stimulate specific physiological changes in the body.

So, even if you don't feel like smiling, smile! The more you *choose* to smile, the more you will feel like smiling. And in the end, the better you will feel overall, both emotionally and physically.

Choose to Be Joyful

Happiness and joy are not the same. Happiness is a feeling of pleasure, contentment, or a sense of well-being that comes from the outer environment or event that a person is experiencing. It is temporary and dependent upon external factors—including what others say and do.

Joy, in contrast, is abiding or enduring. It comes from a feeling of contentment deep inside. It is not dependent on external factors, but on an inner sense of value, purpose, fulfillment, or satisfaction.

Pleasure that produces happiness tends to come through the five senses; for example, eating a delicious chocolate dessert, hearing a beautiful piece of music, or snuggling under a warm, soft blanket. Happiness comes from pleasure-producing perceptions one enjoys while attending an exciting football game, receiving a relaxing massage, hearing a compliment, receiving a gift, finding the perfect item on sale, visiting an amusement park, and so forth.

Happiness-producing pleasures are good; however, they can induce an addiction, and in that regard a person needs to be careful. Drinking, drugs, sex, gambling, eating—almost anything that triggers a pleasure response in a person can become addictive. If your goal is to find happiness through pleasures that are bound to the five senses, you will never be fully satisfied. You will always be looking for more.

There's also a trap associated with happiness. Happiness sometimes comes when we take the path of least resistance, yet it is the tougher, longer, harder pursuits that tend to bring the joy we truly desire.

Marriage is one example. Sometimes people opt for the quick affair, thinking happiness lies in experiencing pleasure wherever they can find it. Marriage is tough work, but studies show that in the long run, those who are married find greater joy and satisfaction in life than those who aren't. Stick with the relationship that has the greater potential for long-term joy.

Likewise, a new home, car, piece of jewelry, or outfit may give a person a temporary feeling of happiness, but these things don't produce long-lasting joy.

Seek out what you believe will really yield long-lasting, abiding joy. Remember, joy does not flow from situations. It flows from your will and your emotions deep within. You can choose to be joyful, or you can choose to be miserable. Nobody can make these inner choices for you.

If you realize that you are not a joyful person, you may want to ask yourself, "Why not?" Some people lose their joy as a consequence of the homes in which they grew up. Some people lose their joy because of exhaustion, burnout, or disappointment. Some people lose their joy because they stop setting goals or making plans. Some people allow a relationship problem to rob them of joy.

Just as a fever is a sign of infection in the body, so the absence of joy—of laughter, humor, or a smile—may be an indication or sign that something is seriously wrong. Psalm 16:11 says, "In Your presence is fullness of joy; at Your right hand are pleasures forevermore." If a person has lost their joy, they have simply stopped entering into God's presence. Through the shed blood of Jesus, we can come boldly to the throne of grace (which is into God's presence). We must enter into His gates with thanksgiving and into His courts with praise. If you have lost the joy in your life, begin praising and thanking God daily, as well as finding other ways to restore it. Here are a few ideas:

Develop a Sense of Play

See what you do as play, not work. Grown-ups can get preoccupied with making money, paying bills, doing chores, meeting challenges, shouldering responsibilities. Children, however, see life as a series of experiences that are enjoyable learning activities or simply fun things to do. Take time regularly to play games with a child. Learn to see the world as the child does. See the antics of the child as being humorous. Become amused at the things that amuse the child. Smile at the things the child smiles at.

Delight in Humorous Stories

I mentioned Victor Frankl in a previous chapter. Frankl was a psychiatrist and survivor of the Auschwitz concentration camp. In his book *Man's Search for Meaning,* he has written that humor was an essential factor in his survival. As a prisoner, he encouraged his fellow prisoners to tell at least one funny story every day about something they intended to do after they were freed. Frankl wrote, "I never would have made it if I could not have laughed."

After he was freed from Auschwitz, Frankl developed a school of psychotherapy called logotherapy, which incorporates humor as a major component of therapy. As a therapist, he encouraged patients to have fun with their problems instead of dealing with them through fighting or fleeing.

Discover Life-Goal Benefits

Find things you enjoy doing, and then do them frequently! Read an interesting novel, get absorbed in a stimulating conversation, spend time with an old friend, work on a hobby. Take time each day to do something that you truly enjoy doing. Usually those activities or causes are ones that you pursue with a passion. Whatever your passionate pursuit, find ways of practicing it frequently.

Have a Purpose, and Pursue It

Gratification comes from the pursuit of something that you believe has meaning and value. What's your reason for getting up in the morning? What keeps you interested in life? What gives you a feeling of fulfillment—a sense that you have done something good for others? Find an outlet for your natural gifts and talents, and then give yourself away to others.

Cut Out the Criticism, Sarcasm, and Negative Jokes

Your parents probably taught you that if people aren't laughing when you are laughing, they very likely perceive that you are laughing at them rather than with them. When one aims to increase, through humor, differences that are cultural, religious, sexual, racial, or political, such humor is nearly always hurtful, not healthful.

If You Are Married, Stay Married

The National Opinion Research Center surveyed thirty-five thousand Americans over a thirty-year period and found that 40 percent of married individuals said they were "very happy." Only 24 percent of unmarried, divorced, separated, or widowed people said they were "happy" or "very happy."[2]

Marriage, more than jobs or finances, is associated with happiness. Marriage is actually one of the strongest predictors of happiness. Studies show that married individuals have the least amount of depression.

Why do I share this information with you? Because as the national divorce rate has increased and marriage has declined in our society, the amount of depression has increased. It certainly would be foolish to suggest that all marriages produce happiness. They don't. On the other hand, those who are in happy, good marriages usually state that there's nothing better in life.

Give Joy Away

How pleasant can you make today? For yourself? For those you love? For total strangers around you? I truly believe that the more you give joy away—including smiles and words of encouragement—the more you will feel joy welling up within. Try it!

FIVE

Learn to Relax

What do you think of when you hear the word *relax-ation*? Though many people think in terms of *unwind-ing*, perhaps a better image would be of *balancing*.

I strongly urge you to clean your plate of things that you do not have to do. I sometimes ask my patients to consider this question: "What would you choose to do, and not do, if you had only six months to live?" Most people quickly come up with a list of things they have to do, things they would like to do, and then a few things they definitely would no longer do. I encourage them to take a look at those things they would no longer do and to drop them from their lives immediately. Then, I recommend that they use that freed-up time and energy to do a few things they would like to do.

So, what would you do if you suddenly realized you had only six months to live? There's a balance of work and rest (including play and recreation) that's right for you. Choose to line up your commitments to achieve that balance.

RELAXATION IS GOOD FOR THE BODY

Every muscle and every organ in the body has a stress state and a relaxed state. Here is a brief look at what happens in the body in each of these states:

Relaxed State	Stressed State
Decrease in heart rate	Increase in heart rate
Decrease in blood pressure	Increase in blood pressure
Increase in digestive function	Decrease in digestive function
Relaxing of blood vessels	Constriction of blood vessels

Does not affect sweat glands	Increases sweating
Increase in oxygen levels	Decrease in oxygen levels
Cellular waste removed	Cellular waste not removed

Clearly, relaxation is good for the body. People have recognized the benefits of relaxation and have used it as a health treatment for thousands of years. You, too, can learn simple methods and practices to generate a relaxation response. All you need is a quiet environment, a positive attitude, and comfortable clothing.

RELAXATION TECHNIQUES

Deep Breathing

Two types of breathing are possible—chest breathing and abdominal breathing. The better of these two is abdominal breathing, which allows more oxygen to get to the muscles. This helps muscles relax. Abdominal breathing has a calming effect on the brain and nervous system, relieving pain and stress.

To learn abdominal breathing, lie down on your back

in a comfortable position with your knees bent. (Once you have learned abdominal breathing, you can perform it standing, sitting, lying down, or moving about.) Next, place your left hand on your abdomen and your right hand on your chest. Notice how your hands move as you breathe in and out. Now try chest breathing so you see the contrast. In chest breathing, the shoulders tend to go up and down with each breath, as opposed to the abdominal cavity moving in and out.

To get into the proper rhythm of abdominal breathing, practice filling your lower lungs. Breathe with an effort at pushing out your left hand and causing your stomach and abdominal cavity area to expand. Your right hand on your chest should remain still. Inhale until you feel your stomach and abdominal cavity expanding to the point of also expanding your chest and rib cage.

Continue breathing this way for a couple of minutes. Make sure your breathing is slow and steady, rising and falling in rhythm. If you have not learned to breathe in this way, you may become dizzy if you get up too quickly. Rise slowly.

Usually a few minutes of abdominal breathing will leave a person feeling relaxed and calm—this amounts to about ten slow, deep, smooth breaths. I instruct my patients to inhale through their noses and exhale through their mouths.

Progressive Muscle Relaxation

Start the technique by tightening a particular muscle group . . . and then relaxing that particular muscle group. Begin doing this by lying or sitting quietly in a comfortable position. Close your eyes. Tighten and relax each muscle group you can identify, beginning at your feet and progressing upward to your face. As you tighten and release muscles, focus on your breathing and practice abdominal breathing. Breathe slowly as you perform this relaxation exercise.

After you have gone from the muscles in your toes to the muscles of your forehead, give yourself a total body check to see if there is any area of your body that still seems to be tight. Redo the clenching and relaxing process in that area.

This total exercise from toe to forehead should take about ten to twenty minutes. When you finish, sit quietly for a few minutes, first with your eyes closed and then with your eyes open. Before you stand up, complete the exercise by raising your hands overhead and stretching them as far as they will go. Simultaneously push your feet out and down as far as they will go. Stretch and slowly count to ten. Repeat this if necessary. If you are under a lot of stress, you may want to practice this technique once or twice a day.

Yoga

A number of different kinds of yoga courses are available. Yoga exercises promote flexibility and strength in the body. They also teach a form of controlled breathing that helps release muscle tension. I do not recommend practicing yoga as a Hindu-related religious practice, which involves various forms of chanting and meditation. I recommend it only as a method of stretching and relaxing.

Visualization and Imagery

We all practice mental imagery and visualization on a daily basis even if we aren't aware that we are doing so. Daydreaming and imagining are visualization techniques.

One visualization exercise is to imagine yourself sitting in a very warm Jacuzzi bath. Feel the pulsating bubbles all around you and the blood flowing to your hands and feet, warming them. Or visualize yourself lying in a warm, flower-covered meadow with a gentle breeze flowing over you and a peaceful brook flowing nearby. Or visualize yourself walking along a beach, with warm, wet sand under your feet and gently lapping waves to your side. Or see yourself sitting on the back porch of a log cabin at night next to a moonlit lake, listening to the crickets chirping and the bullfrogs croaking. Remember to focus on your breathing.

A ten-minute visualization break is like a minivacation: it allows your mind and heart to get away from the stress of the day.

Meditation

Meditation is of two general types. One type is guided meditation, which involves another person asking you to "see" various images on a relaxed journey of some type, perhaps through a forest or across a small footbridge. The other type of meditation aims at emptying the mind of stressful thoughts by focusing on one word, phrase, or a repetitive song. Meditation compels a person to become absorbed in the present moment.

Three different focuses of meditation are common:

1. Concentrated meditation, which requires a person to focus on the sound of his breathing while repeating a meaningful word or phrase or concentrating on a particular mental image.

2. Awareness meditation, which requires a person to focus on a particular feeling or bodily sensation.

3. Expressive meditation, which requires a person to concentrate on a rhythmic physical activity, such as jogging or dancing. A person who is jogging can actually reach a meditative state of calm by concentrating on the up-and-down cadence of his feet striking the pavement.

Meditation has helped people manage chronic pain, relieve insomnia and nausea, and treat substance-abuse disorders. Some studies have shown promise for meditation as a technique for lowering blood pressure and possibly preventing heart attacks.

Prayer

Research has shown prayer to be very useful in inducing the relaxation response. Many individuals seek comfort in prayer during stressful times. Some people use repetitive prayers, such as phrases from the Scriptures that they repeat slowly or the Lord's Prayer. Others find the greatest calm in a complete venting, followed by a time of giving thanks and praise to God.

Some people I know couple praying with reading aloud God's promises from the Bible. Still others couple praying with seeing Jesus as taking a heavy load off their shoulders and strapping it to His own back. These people visualize 1 Peter 5:6–7, which says, "Humble yourselves under the mighty hand of God . . . casting all your care upon Him, for He cares for you."

You can also combine soothing music with meditation, visualization, or prayer. Research has shown that one's religious faith and practices, including prayer, reading Scriptures, and attending worship services, may decrease the impact of emotional stress in daily life and lessen the more serious stress of illness.

Aerobic Exercise

Brisk walking, cycling, swimming, rowing, dancing, jogging, and other aerobic exercises actually help relax the body, provided you do not exercise at too high an intensity.

Massage

One of the oldest health practices is massage. I commonly recommend that my patients have one or two massages a week, especially if they are excessively stressed or have chronic pain, fibromyalgia, or any other disease heavily influenced by stress.

The skin has thousands of receptors that send messages through the nervous system to the brain to induce a feeling of relaxation, comfort, and well-being. Massage can trigger the release of endorphins, which are the body's natural pain relievers. Regular massage can also lower amounts of cortisol and epinephrine, the stress hormones. Massage certainly is helpful in releasing muscle tension, which can help with circulation.

Sleep: The Ultimate Relaxation Time

Too many Americans today are living in a sleep-deprived state. Physical stress and, ultimately, stress-related diseases are the consequences. It is also critically important that you sleep seven to nine hours a night. Aim for eight to nine hours of sleep on weekend nights.

Here are some simple suggestions for improving your sleep:

Limit your bedroom to sleep. By limiting this room to sleep only, you send a signal to your body that entering this room begins the go-to-sleep process of unwinding and relaxing.

Go to bed and get up at approximately the same time each day. Do this even on weekends. This regular routine conditions your internal clock.

Keep your bedroom uncluttered. This will help you avoid distractions that may cause stress.

Keep your bedroom dark. Make sure that no light shines in from the street or even from a nightlight. You may need to cover up a bright digital clock. Start dimming the lights in other rooms of your house in early evening.

Shut off the noisemakers. Unplug the phone in your bedroom. Use earplugs if necessary to keep honking horns or sirens from interrupting your sleep. (On stormy nights, however, you may want to leave out the earplugs so you can hear a storm-warning siren.)

Do not drink beverages with caffeine in the evening (coffee, tea, soft drinks). Also don't eat chocolate, spicy foods, or fatty foods before bedtime. And avoid medications containing caffeine or stimulants in the evening.

Keep your bedroom at a comfortable temperature. For

most people this is around seventy degrees Fahrenheit.

Don't exercise just before bedtime. Do your exercise in the late afternoon or early evening, but not within two hours of bedtime.

Select a comfortable pillow and mattress. Use a mattress that allows you to sleep soundly with good body support for your spine.

Practice a relaxation technique prior to bedtime. It is important to "wind down" before going to bed. Slow down and relax by dimming the lights, taking a soothing bath with lavender oil, and playing soft, relaxing music. If you do awaken in the night, get up only if you absolutely must. If you have trouble falling back to sleep, try a relaxation technique as you lie in bed. You may want to memorize and then recite Scripture verses if you awaken in the night:

- I will both lie down in peace, and sleep; for You alone, O LORD, make me dwell in safety. (Ps. 4:8)
- It is vain for you to rise up early, to sit up late, to eat the bread of sorrows; for so He gives His beloved sleep. (Ps. 127:2)
- When you lie down, you will not be afraid; yes,

you will lie down and your sleep will be sweet.
(Prov. 3:24)

Keep the Sabbath day. A time of prolonged rest during
daylight hours is also part of God's plan for the human
body. Many people seem to think they are honoring the
Sabbath by not going into the workplace, but in reality,
they work on that day by shopping or doing house- or
yardwork. God intended the Sabbath to be a time of
quiet and peaceful meditation and conversation about
God's Word—a time with family and close friends, void
of hurry, work, or any activities that require prolonged
mental or physical exertion.

RELAX REGULARLY

Even if you aren't feeling particularly stressed right now,
begin to practice relaxation response techniques regularly
to avoid getting stressed. I have found in my practice that
the specific technique a patient uses isn't as important as
the fact that he practices relaxation daily. Choose the
technique that works best for you, and use it regularly.

Then when a stressful situation hits you, you will know how to respond quickly and effectively to counteract a stress buildup.

Regular relaxation helps a person perform better, work better, give more, accomplish more, be open to laughing more, and experience inner peace. If you learn to relax, you will be in a position to experience much greater health.

SIX

Express Love

Mother Teresa said that the greatest disease of mankind is the absence of love. I couldn't agree more. I believe an ability to love begins in receiving God's love—usually in the form of His mercy and forgiveness—and then learning to love ourselves.

LOVING YOURSELF

How do you love yourself? In many ways, this relates to self-esteem—to having feelings of worthiness, value, and purpose in life. In the physical realm, the way we generally show love to our bodies is to pamper them. Touch is an important part of this. I don't know anybody who doesn't enjoy a good back, foot, or neck rub, especially after a high-stress day. We human beings enjoy the sensation of being touched in a gentle, loving, and stimulating way. We enjoy human contact, but we also enjoy the feelings we have through the nerve endings of our skin.

However, truly loving yourself means accepting and forgiving yourself unconditionally every day in spite of what you have or haven't done. It means not comparing yourself to others, and refusing to blame, criticize, or condemn yourself. It involves speaking kindly to yourself and realizing that you are special. You are a child of the King and the righteousness of God in Christ.

Whatever feelings that you have toward yourself are generally going to be projected onto other people. You will generally love others to the degree that you love yourself. You will accept and trust others to the degree that you accept yourself. You will forgive others to the degree that you forgive yourself. Matthew 22:39 says, "You shall love your neighbor as yourself." You are not only commanded to love your neighbor but also commanded to love yourself.

EXPERIENCING GENUINE, HEALING LOVE

Many people in our society place a high emphasis on romantic love. Yet the kind of love that truly heals us emotionally and physically is not romantic love but the unconditional love that comes from God.

How can we tell if we are experiencing genuine love in our lives? One of the most eloquent love descriptions of all time appears in 1 Corinthians:

> Love suffers long and is kind; love does not envy; love does not parade itself, is not puffed up; does not behave rudely, does not seek its own, is not provoked, thinks no evil; does not rejoice in iniquity, but rejoices in the truth; bears all things, believes all things, hopes all things, endures all things. Love never fails . . .
>
> And now abide faith, hope, love, these three; but the greatest of these is love. (1 Cor. 13:4–8, 13)

Let me briefly comment on the hallmark characteristics of love that Paul mentions.

Love Is Patient

Do you suffer from "hurry sickness" or impatience? A simple test of patience: how long does it take for you to honk your horn when you are sitting behind a driver who does not move after the light turns green? A truly patient person seldom honks, and if he does, it is usually with a gentle reminder tap. An impatient person is quick to lay on the horn.

Love Is Kind

Kind people touch others—literally and figuratively—including those that others may perceive as untouchable. How quick are you to give a smile, your time, gifts, joy, and a listening ear to others?

Love Is Not Jealous

It does not seek to control or manipulate others. Are you willing to allow others to share friendship with your friends? Are you quick to volunteer your possessions or your home for something that benefits others? Are you quick to applaud others who succeed or who are promoted or receive rewards?

Love Is Not Proud or Boastful

Do you feel an overwhelming need to tell others about your achievements or possessions? Does the conversation always seem to come around to you—not because others ask but because you feel a need to tell?

Love Is Not Rude

One of the great manifestations of love is courtesy. Unloving people rarely care about manners, and they don't bother saying "please" or "thank you." How about you?

Love Is Not Selfish

Selfish people are those who insist on having their way. They expect others to give in to their demands. They are "my way or the highway" people. Are you quick to put the needs of others ahead of your needs?

Love Does Not Keep Track of Wrongs

Loving people forgive quickly and easily and refuse to keep score against another person. Check your own heart. Are you holding something against another person? Do you feel you need to settle a score with someone? It's plain and simple—if you can't forgive yourself or others, then you *can't* love.

Love Is Quick to Believe the Best

Love doesn't gossip or look for flaws in other people. Love holds people in high regard and quickly overlooks a mistake. Do you often jump to the worst conclusions about people without giving them the benefit of the doubt?

Love Desires Justice

Those who are loving want to see justice prevail for those who are victims. They find no pleasure in hearing about crime or violence. They have hearts that desire to help the innocent. Is there anybody about whom you find yourself saying, "He deserved what he got"?

Love Never Fails

Love is constant, and we are promised that it *never* fails. The truly loving person just keeps on loving, no matter what happens—no matter what others say or do, or the situation or circumstances. Love hangs in there. Have you given up on a person, convinced that she is destined for hard times or eternal punishment?

MAKING THE CHOICE
TO BE LOVING

Walking in love is a choice. Acting on that choice takes effort. Love means choosing to turn yourself inside out for others, to turn your thinking upside down from the way the vast majority of people in the world think, and to go radically against what many people perceive to be basic human nature and pursue instead the nature of God. A person who makes a commitment to walk in love is a person who nearly always discovers he has made a decision of supreme quality.

EXPRESSING HEALING LOVE
TO OTHERS

It is not enough that you feel love in your heart. You must give away love. We do this in several basic ways.

Words of affirmation to others. Be quick to give compliments or encouraging words in response to what another person does or says. Especially with children, be sure to balance constructive criticism with words of praise and encouragement. It generally takes ten words of praise to offset one word of criticism.

The gift of time. There's an old saying that children spell love t-i-m-e. The same is true for spouses. Spending time with a person, without an agenda or task to accomplish, is love expressed.

The giving of gifts. Find out what another person likes and then give that gift.

Acts of service. Service is different from gift-giving. In gifts, the focus is on what brings pleasure to a person. Service focuses on what a person truly needs. What can you do to help the busiest person you love? The answer is likely an act of service: fixing dinner, mowing the lawn, picking up the laundry, or taking a package to the post office.

Acts of physical affection. We are human beings who need touch. An act of love may be as simple as a kiss, hug, caress, pat on the back, or holding hands. It may be sexual intercourse with a spouse, or a long massage or back rub. We touch those we truly love—and always in a way that the other person perceives to be appropriate.

It isn't enough that we choose to express love in these ways. What's truly important is that we discover which expressions of love our loved ones most desire and most readily receive. Which form of love expression does the person you love seem to need or request most often?

The Bible includes Paul's desire for followers of Christ: "May the Lord make you increase and abound in love to one another and to all, just as we do to you, so that He may establish your hearts blameless in holiness before our God and Father at the coming of our Lord Jesus Christ with all his saints" (1 Thess. 3:12–13). That's my hope for you.

SEVEN

Eat Right and Exercise

In 1901, the United States was classified as the healthiest nation in the world among one hundred nations studied. By 1920, we had dropped to second place. By 1950, we were in third place. By 1970, we were in forty-first place. And in 1981, we had dropped all the way to ninety-fifth place![1]

How does a nation go from being first place in the area of good health to ninety-fifth place in just one century? The answer can be summed up in two words: *diet* and *exercise*. Eating right and exercising are essential to stress management and good health.

EAT A MEDITERRANEAN DIET

I am a strong advocate of the Mediterranean Diet and have written a book on the subject titled *What Would Jesus Eat?* The foods that Jesus ate are very similar to those advocated in the Mediterranean Diet (with the exception of the forbidden foods listed in the books of Leviticus and Deuteronomy). Numerous research studies have indicated that it is the healthiest diet in the world.

The benefits of the Mediterranean Diet have been known for almost forty years. They include a decreased risk of coronary heart disease; a decreased incidence of cancers (other than lung cancer or cigarette-related cancers), hypertension, obesity, and most other degenerative diseases; and a longer life expectancy.

Basically, the American diet is too high in saturated fats, sugar, processed food, salt, red meat, and fast foods—and conversely, too low in fresh fruits, vegetables, and whole grains. The Mediterranean Diet has a much better balance.

Here is the food guide pyramid for the Mediterranean Diet:

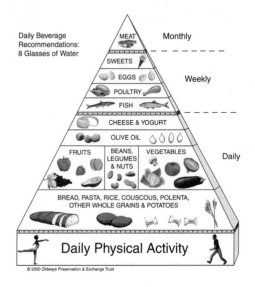

Daily Beverage
Recommendations:
8 Glasses of Water

MEAT — Monthly

SWEETS

EGGS — Weekly

POULTRY

FISH

CHEESE & YOGURT

OLIVE OIL

FRUITS | BEANS, LEGUMES & NUTS | VEGETABLES — Daily

BREAD, PASTA, RICE, COUSCOUS, POLENTA, OTHER WHOLE GRAINS & POTATOES

Daily Physical Activity

© 2000 Oldways Preservation & Exchange Trust

The Mediterranean Diet emphasizes unprocessed foods. Complex carbohydrates are at the base. These foods include brown rice or whole-grain pasta, and whole-grain bread (ideally, prepared without preservatives). Other grains appropriate for the base of this pyramid are bulgur wheat (cracked whole wheat), couscous, polenta (coarse cornmeal), and potatoes. In Mediterranean nations, where whole-grain breads are consumed with each meal, the whole-grains have a high amount of fiber without excessive sugars, hydrogenated fats, or food additives.

At the next level are fruits, vegetables, beans, other legumes, and nuts. A typical meal includes a salad of dark green leafy lettuce and fresh vegetables. Fresh vegetables also are served with pasta or rice, as appetizers, or as a side or main dish. Fruit is eaten mainly as a dessert or snack.

Legumes and beans are generally served in soups or added to salads, and are even offered as a main course. Nuts are often added to salads or to main dishes, and are not usually consumed by themselves.

The third level in the pyramid is olive oil, which is used in place of margarine, butter, shortening, and other oils. It is used in cooking as well as combined with balsamic vinegar to make a salad dressing.

The fourth level is cheese and yogurt. The diet uses very small amounts of cheese, such as Parmesan cheese on pasta and feta cheese on a salad. Milk is generally not consumed as a beverage but eaten in the form of low or nonfat yogurt, served plain or with fresh fruit.

Fish, the fifth level, is consumed far more frequently than red meat or poultry. Eating four-ounce portions of fish several times a week is very beneficial.

Poultry and eggs are at the sixth level. The diet includes three ounces of chicken two to four times a week. Average egg consumption in these nations is from zero to four eggs a week. Generally, they are not a staple breakfast item but are used in the making of bread and desserts.

At the seventh level are sweets, typically saved as "treats" for birthdays, weddings, and other celebrations.

The top of the pyramid is devoted to red meat, which includes meat from beef, veal, pork, sheep, lamb, and goats. Red meat is rarely consumed more than a few times a month in Mediterranean nations and generally is mixed with large amounts of vegetables, pasta, and rice. This meat tends to be reserved for special occasions and is stewed or baked.

Mediterranean meals are usually served with red wine or bottled water, and rarely is more than one glass (four ounces) consumed at a meal.

MAKING THE CHANGE

To change from a typical American way of eating to a Mediterranean one:

1. Eliminate all processed foods from your cupboards and start over. This includes any salad dressings, lard, Crisco, and other products that have hydrogenated fat.
2. Cook and bake with whole-grain products. Eat more fresh fruits and vegetables, beans, legumes, and nuts.
3. Substitute organic extra-virgin olive oil for butter, margarine, salad dressings, and other oils. Avoid all fried or deep-fried foods.
4. Limit cheese intake to small amounts of Parmesan or feta cheese (used on main dishes or salads).
5. Eat lowfat plain yogurt, add fruit, and sweeten it with Stevia (a natural sugar substitute) or agave nectar (available at health food stores).
6. Choose fish and poultry over red meat, and eat meat sparingly.
7. Cut out sugary sweets.
8. Slow down your eating, savor your food, and enjoy talking with family and friends.
9. Exercise regularly—walk more.
10. Drink eight glasses of pure water a day.

EXERCISE REGULARLY

More than half of all American adults are either overweight or obese, and approximately 25 percent of our children are either overweight or obese. Obesity is a risk factor for heart disease, hypertension, diabetes, arthritis, some forms of cancer, and other degenerative diseases. Both diet and exercise are essential to a healthy lifestyle.

Some of the many benefits of regular physical exercise include the following:

- promotes psychological well-being
- reduces stress and anxiety
- helps maintain ideal weight and improve muscle tone
- improves cardiovascular capacity, increasing energy and promoting more restful sleep
- increases the flow of lymphatic fluid, eliminating cellular waste and LDL (bad) cholesterol
- increases perspiration, which rids the body of waste products
- improves circulation to the skin, nourishing and rejuvenating the skin and removing cellular waste
- improves digestion and elimination

- increases the frequency of bowel movements (when combined with adequate water intake)
- lowers the risk of developing blood clots

In fact, few things can do more to promote good health than adequate physical activity—especially exercise that is aerobic.

AEROBIC EXERCISE

The most beneficial cardiovascular activity is aerobic exercise, which challenges and increases the oxygen-carrying capacity of the body. Aerobic exercises use the large muscle groups of the body in repetitive motions for a sustained period of time, such as brisk walking, jogging, aerobic dancing, cycling, swimming, rowing, stair-stepping, skating, and cross-country skiing. An aerobic effect can also be gained by playing a vigorous game of singles tennis, basketball, or another active sport.

Even moderately paced walking is an excellent form of aerobic exercise. In fact, some research shows that moderately paced walking five times a week for thirty minutes is just as advantageous as brisk walking or jogging, although the benefits from a brisk walk or jog can be achieved in less time.

The greatest benefit of aerobic exercise is that it significantly decreases the risk of cardiovascular disease—up to 50 percent. For those with heart disease, aerobic exercise lowers the risk of the disease progressing. It also decreases what are called *coronary risk factors,* which seem to impact heart disease. Specifically, it helps decrease body weight, lower blood pressure, lower blood triglyceride levels, lower LDL (bad) cholesterol, and raise HDL (good) cholesterol.

Regular aerobic exercise also helps prevent diabetes, improve glucose tolerance, and improve the body's ability to use insulin, as well as decrease the risk of developing cancer.

WEIGHT-BEARING EXERCISE

Studies have shown that weight-bearing exercises, which include jogging, aerobic dance, and walking, help a person maintain bone density and thereby prevent osteoporosis.

Dr. Kenneth Cooper, considered to be the founder of the aerobic exercise movement, is a strong advocate for impact-type exercises, which increase bone density in both men and women in skeletal areas that are subjected to the increased pressure from impact exercises.

STARTING AN EXERCISE PROGRAM

The most important exercise that almost everyone can perform on a regular basis is walking. The only equipment required is a good pair of walking shoes. But if you don't enjoy walking, find an exercise you do enjoy. By doing what you enjoy, you are likely to engage in the exercise more often and for a sustained amount of time.

Experts recommend twenty to thirty minutes of aerobic exercise three to four days a week. I recommend you *schedule* a half-hour appointment three to four days a week for exercise. Write it down in your day planner or on an appointment calendar. Then keep the appointment!

The total thirty minutes of exercise do not necessarily need to be done at one time. A fifteen-minute walk at the start of the lunch hour and a fifteen-minute walk an hour before dinner result in similar benefits to a thirty-minute concentrated period of exercise.

It is best, however, to schedule your exercise time during the midafternoon to early evening hours. I recommend you exercise at least an hour before the evening meal to help release the tensions of the day, suppress your appetite, and gain energy for the evening's activities. I also recommend you do not exercise too late at night so that an increased energy level does not keep you from falling asleep readily.

You probably will find it much easier to maintain an exercise program if you are accountable to another person. Recruit a family member or friend to exercise with you regularly, or join an exercise group or class. The important thing is to start, and then to continue exercising on a regular basis. Make exercise a priority.

Here are some basic guidelines for starting an exercise program:

1. Undergo a thorough medical exam prior to starting an exercise program.
2. Exercise for thirty minutes three to four times a week.

3. A well-rounded exercise program includes aerobic exercise, stretching, and resistance or weight training. Note: For weight reduction, it is usually best to perform weight-training exercise prior to aerobic exercise.

4. Always stretch prior to exercising.

5. Exercise smart; know your target heart rate.

6. Don't be a "weekend warrior," risking injury and overexertion. Two to three hours of solid exercise on the weekend are not the same as thirty minutes of exercise three to four times a week.

7. Begin slowly and increase your pace gradually to warm up your muscles. Slow your pace a few minutes before ending as a cooldown.

CONSISTENCY AND COMMITMENT

There is no question that eating right and exercising regularly improve health and reduce stress. In fact, for complete and total health, you cannot have one without the other. We know this to be true, yet most of us fail to eat the right foods consistently or get sufficient exercise regularly. Often we change our diet or begin an exercise program but fail to sustain either. When it comes to diet and exercise, we must follow a three-step plan: 1) Start doing what we know we should do; 2) Do it regularly; and 3) Keep doing it!

If you want to manage the stress in your life and lead a healthier life, you cannot ignore your eating and exercising habits. Adopting the practices in this chapter—and those suggested throughout this book—requires a commitment to change, a commitment to be all that God created you to be, and a commitment to yield your desires to God's instruction. God, in turn, will honor your heartfelt commitment by giving you more energy, better health, inner peace, and a greater sense of well-being.

The choice is yours. *Choose* health!

Notes

Introduction

1. D. Wayne, "Reactions to Stress," found in Identifying Stress, a series offered by the Health-Net & Stress Management Web site, February 1998.

Chapter 2

1. Live interview from the American Psychological Association 108th Convention, Washington, DC, moderator Frank Farley (6 August 2000).

Chapter 4

1. C. A. Anderson and L. H. Arnault, "An Examination of Perceived Control, Humor,

Irrational Beliefs, and Positive Stress as Moderators of the Relation Between Negative Stress and Health," *Basic and Applied Social Psychology,* 10 (1989): 101–17.

2. David G. Myers and Ed Diener, "In Pursuit of Happiness," *Scientific American,* May 1996.

Chapter 7

1. Gunther B. Paulien, Ph.D, *The Divine Philosophy and Science of Health and Healing* (Brushton, NY: Teach Services, Inc., 1995), 202.

About the Author

DON COLBERT, M.D., a board-certified family practitioner since 1987, is the author of such best sellers as *What Would Jesus Eat?*, *Toxic Relief*, *Walking in Divine Health*, The Bible Cure Booklet Series, *What You Don't Know May Be Killing You*, and *Stress Less*. He writes monthly columns for *Charisma* magazine and Joyce Meyers's *Partners* magazine. Dr. Colbert developed his own vitamin line, Divine Health Nutritional Products, and hosts a national talk show titled *Your Health Matters* with his wife, Mary. He regularly speaks at national seminars on such topics as "The Dangers of Stress" and "The Seven Pillars of Health." He makes his home in the Orlando, Florida area. For more information, visit www.drcolbert.com.

About the Author

DON COLBERT, M.D., a board-certified family practitioner since 1987, is the author of such best sellers as *What Would Jesus Eat?*, *Toxic Relief*, *Walking in Divine Health*, The Bible Cure Booklet Series, *What You Don't Know May Be Killing You*, and *Stress Less*. He writes monthly columns for *Charisma* magazine and Joyce Meyers's *Partners* magazine. Dr. Colbert developed his own vitamin line, Divine Health Nutritional Products, and hosts a national talk show titled *Your Health Matters* with his wife, Mary. He regularly speaks at national seminars on such topics as "The Dangers of Stress" and "The Seven Pillars of Health." He makes his home in the Orlando, Florida area. For more information, visit www.drcolbert.com.